D1123519

small worlds

A RAIN FOREST TREE

Lorien Kite

CRABTREE
Publishing Company

Crabtree Publishing Company

350 Fifth Avenue
Suite 3308
New York, NY 10118

360 York Road, R.R.4
Niagara-on-the-Lake
Ontario LOS 1J0

Co-ordinating editor: Ellen Rodger
Commissioning editor: Anne O'Daly
Editor: Clare Oliver
Designer: Joan Curtis
Picture researcher: Christine Lalla
Consultants: Staff of the Natural History Museum, London
and David T. Brown PhD

Illustrator: Peter Bull

Photographs: Jim Clarke/BBC Natural History Unit p 20 *inset*; John Downer/BBC Natural History Unit p 7*t*; Tim Edwards /BBC Natural History Unit p 11*b*; Gerry Ellis/BBC Natural History Unit pp 13*t*, 13*b*, 16*t*, 26*t*; Nick Gordon/BBC Natural History Unit p 28; Pete Oxford/BBC Natural History Unit pp 16*b*, 24*t*, 29; Morley Read/BBC Natural History Unit pp 12*t*, 22*b*, 29; Phil Savoie/BBC Natural History Unit pp 11*t*, 18*t*; Lynn M Stone/BBC Natural History Unit p 23*t*; Doug Wechsler/BBC Natural History Unit pp 8*m*, 21*b*, 25; Gunter Ziesler/Bruce Coleman Limited p 12*b*; Wolfgang Kaehler/Corbis Images p 7*m*; Michael and Patricia Fogden/Corbis Images p 24*b*; Michael and Patricia Fogden, front and back cover, pp 3, 5, 7*b*, 8*t*, 9, 10*t*, 14, 17, 18*b*, 19, 20, 22*t*, 27; James Carmichael/Imagebank, front cover, pp 1, 15, 23*b*; Deborah Gilbert/Imagebank p 31; Silvestris Fotoservice/NHPA p 21*t*; Harry Smith Horicultural Photographic Collection p 30.

Created and produced by
Brown Partworks Ltd

First edition 1999
10 9 8 7 6 5 4 3 2 1

CATALOGING-IN-PUBLICATION DATA

Kite, Lorien, 1973-
    A rain forest tree / Lorien Kite. — 1st ed.
    p. cm. — (Small worlds)
Includes index.
    SUMMARY: Describes the plants and animals that live at the different levels—canopy, understory, and floor—in a rain forest.
    ISBN 0-7787-0132-8 (rlb)
    ISBN 0-7787-0146-8 (pbk.)
    1. Rain forest ecology—Juvenile literature. 2. Rain forests—Juvenile literature. [1. Rain forests. 2. Rain forest ecology. 3. Ecology.] I. Title. II. Series: Small worlds.
    QH541.5.R27 K58 1999
    577.34—dc21

                                                    LC 98-51709
                                                    CIP
                                                    AC

Printed in Singapore

Contents

Rain forests around the world   4

Life in a rain forest tree   6

Life in the canopy   8

Understory life   18

Life on the forest floor   24

Life in a tree near you   30

Words to know   32

Index   32

Rain forests around the world

Tropical rain forests grow wherever it is warm and wet all year round. They are home to more animals and plants than any habitat on Earth.

No plant or animal species is found in every single rain forest, but creatures living in forests far, far apart are often very similar. African leopards, South and Central American jaguars, and Asian tigers are all large cats that hunt in the lower levels of the forest.

In this book, you will meet the plants and animals that live in a South American rain forest tree. You will see how they depend on one another. You will discover how each plays its part in the life of the forest.

▲ *Apes and monkeys are found in rain forests around the world. Spider monkeys live in South America.*

▶ *A tropical rain forest is hot and steamy.*

▶ *There are tropical rain forests (shown in red) in Central and South America, Africa, India, Southeast Asia, and Northeast Australia.*

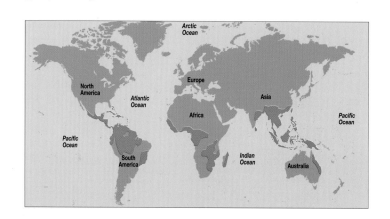

Life in a rain forest tree

Tropical rain forests are home to more than half of the different kinds of plants and animals on Earth.

Rain forest trees can be over 200 feet (61 m) tall. They divide into layers, like the stories of a building. The top branches get lots of sun. The layers get darker as you go down. Different plants and animals live in each layer.

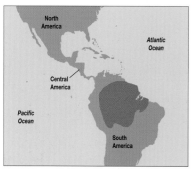

The Amazon rain forest (in red) is in South America.

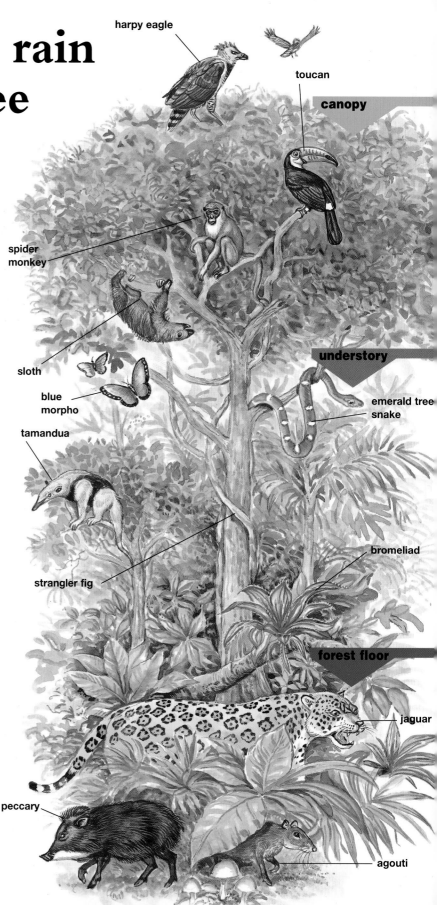

6

Life in the canopy

This is where the trees spread their branches to form a crowded, leafy roof over the forest. Many plants and animals are found here. Sloths munch on leaves, monkeys leap from branch to branch in search of fruit, and the air is full of brightly colored birds and butterflies. Insects, tree frogs, and lizards hide among the leaves.

Understory life

The understory is shaded from the sun by the leaves of the canopy. Here, straight, branchless trunks tower up toward the light. Orchids grow from cracks in the bark. Tree ferns and palms brush their leaves against the giant tree trunks. Snakes, cats, and anteaters can all be found in the understory.

Life on the forest floor

Little light reaches the forest floor. This is the gloomiest part of the forest. Fungi love the damp darkness, and there is a smell of decay in the air. Animals of the forest floor include jaguars, tapirs, and peccaries. Forest peoples can be found here, too, hunting monkeys and birds from the canopy with poison darts.

Life in the canopy

This barred tree frog is clinging to a branch in the canopy.

The canopy is the level where the treetops join together. Some of the animals living here never come down to the ground.

Only a few giant trees poke higher than the top of the canopy.

The canopy is where the giant rain forest trees unfurl their leaves to soak up the sun. Trees need the sun's energy to make leaves and seeds. Some trees even turn their leaves to follow the sun as it moves across the sky!

Almost every day, heavy rainstorms drench the canopy. In these warm, moist conditions,

One of the biggest and slowest leaf-eaters in the canopy is the sloth. To save energy, it sleeps 16 hours a day!

Many leaves have drip tips—tiny spouts that allow the rainwater to run off.

moss and algae thrive. They coat every branch and even grow on some of the leaves. A tree would die if too many of its leaves were covered from the light, so canopy leaves have smooth, waxy surfaces that are too slippery for moss and algae to grow on.

The secret world of a bromeliad

Bromeliads are epiphytes—plants that rest on the branches of trees and hang their roots in the air. A bromeliad plant is a busy place! Many insects hide beneath its leaves, so lizards and birds often stop by looking for a tasty meal. In the center of the leaves is a tiny pool of rainwater, where the larvae (babies) of mosquitoes and beetles live. Many tree frogs lay their eggs here, and their tadpoles hatch in the pools of water.

A room at the top

The massive branches of rain forest trees are also home to **epiphytes**. Epiphytes are plants that grow high up from the ground and collect moisture by dangling their roots in the damp air. Many have developed ways of collecting extra rainwater. For example, the bromeliad plant channels rain and dew into a central cup with its upward-pointing, overlapping leaves.

*▲ Epiphytes draw their **nutrients** from the decayed remains of algae, moss, and leaves.*

▼ The roots of this strangler fig have snaked down and around the trunk of the host tree.

The forest strangler

The strangler fig starts life as an epiphyte in the canopy but sends its roots all the way down the trunk of the tree it lives on. Once its roots are buried in the forest floor, the fig can suck up lots more water, which helps it grow quickly. The strangler fig sends down more roots and shoots out more branches until it blocks out all the light for the tree it lives on. By the time the tree dies, the fig's thick roots have formed a new trunk.

The katydid looks like a creature from outer space, but it is a type of grasshopper! It feeds on leaves and small insects.

Leaf-munchers

For many insects and some large **mammals**, the leaves of the canopy are an endless supply of food. Even though some of the leaves are poisonous, most leaf-eaters can eat the poisoned leaves of the tree they live on. Some insects even use the poison to their advantage. They store it in their bodies to stop **predators** from eating them.

Fruit bats love to feast on sugary fruit. The night-flying bats follow the smell of the fruit to find a meal in the dark.

Fruity business

The highest trees in the forest spread their light seeds in the wind, but for most of the trees in the canopy, wind-power is not an option. Beneath the very highest branches, the air is perfectly still. These trees have seeds surrounded by sweet, juicy fruit. The fruit tempts bats, birds, monkeys, and other creatures. The fruit-eating animals swallow the seeds with the fruit. Large seeds are coughed up, often some distance from the parent tree. Small seeds pass right through an animal's digestive system. The seeds then sprout from the animal's droppings, which provide a rich, ready-made fertilizer!

Fruit often appeals to a particular kind of animal. Monkeys grab the fruit that sprouts from medium-sized branches, while birds snatch berries that hang from the thinnest twigs. Some trees make fruit that drops to the forest floor as soon as it ripens. This fruit is eaten by large, ground-dwelling mammals.

These cashew nuts might attract the attention of a passing bird or a very light and nimble monkey.

Say it with flowers

Before they can make seeds and fruit, trees and other plants need to be **fertilized**. This happens when **pollen**, a fine yellow powder produced by the male parts of flowers, is carried from one flower to another of the same species. Animals, especially insects, act as pollen carriers.

Animals are attracted to flowers by **nectar**, a sweet and highly nutritious food. As the animals sip the nectar, pollen grains brush onto their bodies. When the animals go on to visit a flower of the same species, they fertilize it accidentally. Different tree species form partnerships with different animals. Sweet-smelling flowers are designed to attract insects.

The passion vine climbs up trees of the forest. Its flowers have bright petals that stand out from the background of a tree trunk and attract animal visitors.

A hummingbird hovers in mid-air, sipping nectar from a flower. The tiniest birds in the forest, some hummingbirds are no bigger than a bumblebee.

Brightly colored flowers attract birds, which have good vision but no sense of smell. These plants do not need to produce perfumes. Some flowers have developed so that their nectar can only be reached by one creature in the forest.

Big bird

Of all the rain forest's creatures, birds are the best suited to life in the treetops. There are more species, or kinds, of birds in tropical South America than anywhere else in the world. Not all birds are content to drink nectar. Many eat insects, lizards, and small mammals. Right at the top of the canopy's food chain are the harpy eagles, the largest birds in the forest.

The food chain

Food chains show how living things depend on each other. Plants are at the start of the chain. They make their own food from sunlight and water. Plant eaters are animals such as sloths that eat leaves, fruit, or nectar. Plant eaters are eaten by carnivores, animals that eat other animals, which are the next step in the chain.

plants

plant eaters

carnivores

Harpy eagles are huge, powerful birds that eat animals as big as monkeys and sloths. Harpy eagles swoop silently down to snatch up their **prey** in their razor-sharp talons.

All kinds of noise

The forest canopy is a noisy place. It is so densely packed with leaves and branches that animals cannot see very far. Instead, many forest animals use sound to communicate with others of their kind. In the forest canopy, the air is thick with screeches, howls, rattles, grunts, croaks, and clicks.

Parrots live in large flocks. They search for food together and warn each other when danger approaches.

Howler monkeys are the noisiest of all the creatures in the rain forest. Their calls can travel two miles (3.2 km) through the air.

Moving around

The animals of the canopy are specially adapted to life in the trees. Many insects, lizards, and mammals have sharp claws that grip the rough bark. Frogs use their sticky feet to cling to tree branches.

Monkeys are the champion climbers of the rain forest. They travel far and wide in search of their favorite food, fruit, and they rarely come down to the ground. Monkeys can grab branches with their hands, feet, or tails. Some species can leap across gaps of 30 feet (9 m).

▲ *Howler monkeys mark their territory by screeching loudly each morning.*

▶ *Tree frogs have sticky suction pads on their toes to hold on to slippery branches.*

16

A prehensile tail

A tail that can grasp is called **prehensile**. Many creatures of the South American rain forest have prehensile tails, including monkeys, opossums, climbing porcupines, and anteaters. Prehensile tails give an animal five limbs to climb with. The animal can anchor itself firmly to a branch with its tail, leaving its hands free to pick fruit, eat insects, or fight off attackers.

Understory life

Between the brightly lit canopy and the dark forest floor is a layer of smaller trees known as the understory.

▲ *Eyelash vipers and other snakes slink through the trees.*

▶ *The see-through wings of glasswing butterflies make them almost invisible in the tree shade.*

In the understory, the hanging roots of figs dangle in mid-air, while lianas and creeping vines coil upward. Only a little light filters through the canopy, so plants here have to make the most of it. Palms and tree ferns have huge leaves, which can be up to three feet (0.9 m) long.

▶ *The branchless trunks of canopy trees tower up toward the light.*

Lianas: ladders in the forest

Lianas are woody plants that rely on trees for support. They cling to saplings, or young trees, on the forest floor and grow with them until they reach the canopy. Lianas live longer than many large trees, and when their host tree dies, they will often start climbing up another. For many climbing mammals, such as the white uakari monkey shown above, lianas act as ladders between the forest floor and the canopy!

The tamandua's long, snouty nose is perfect for thrusting into a nest to suck up a tasty meal.

There is less plant life in the understory, and fewer creatures live here. It is still busy with animals climbing up and down the lianas or swinging on the vines.

Home-breaker

The tamandua, or lesser anteater, is always searching for a meal.

Termites build their nests using a mixture of chewed wood and their own saliva.

Tamanduas live mainly on termites, ant-like insects that can be found all over the rain forest. Termites build rock-hard nests on the sides of trees. Tamanduas have huge, sharp claws and can break into these insect fortresses. The animals' spiky tongues dart in and out of the hole they make, slurping up insects as they go.

FANTASTIC FACTS

● Some lianas are over 3,500 feet (1,000 m) long.

● Tamanduas can thrust their tongues in and out of a termite nest at a rate of 160 strokes a minute!

▶ *This chestnut-mandibled toucan uses its long curved beak to pick and eat fruit. A toucan's beak can be over seven inches (17.8 cm) long.*

Birds fly from tree to tree beneath the canopy, safe from eagles patrolling the skies. Many birds raise their chicks here too, nesting inside rotten tree trunks. The hope of a tasty, defenceless meal brings monkeys and hawks down from the treetops. Snakes, weasels, and coatimundis (small mammals) venture up from the forest floor in search of eggs and chicks.

▼ *Snakes are among the quietest hunters of the understory. They slither noiselessly upon their prey. This rattlesnake's mottled black and yellow skin blends in with the tree bark.*

Climbing cats such as the ocelot, the jaguarundi, and the margay prey on small birds, mice, and lizards. They are well **camouflaged**, with spotted yellow and black coats that seem to disappear in the dappled sunlight.

The jaguar is larger and stockier than its African cousin, the leopard. Like the leopard, it lies in wait for its prey in the trees— and then pounces!

A colorful world

Many rainforest animals are brightly colored. Poisonous frogs and insects are often blue, red, or yellow. Their color is a warning to other animals not to eat them. Some harmless creatures copy these colors, so that they won't be eaten either!

The feathers of many birds blend with colors of plants in the forest. Bright green birds disappear against the leaves of the forest, while red, white, or yellow ones are easily mistaken for fruits or flowers. Color also helps birds to recognize one another.

Life on the forest floor

Little light reaches the forest floor, so few plants grow here. The rotting piles of leaves make an ideal home for insects and fungi.

▲ *Rain forest tarantulas can be up to three inches (7.6 cm) long. They eat insects, mice, and even small birds!*

▶ *The horned frog has the perfect disguise to avoid being spotted on the forest floor. It looks just like leaf litter.*

Underneath the **leaf litter**, the soil is thin and lacking in nutrients, so the trees do not put down deep roots. Instead, they send their roots along or just beneath the ground, sucking nutrients from the rotting leaves.

▶ *The floor of the rain forest is covered with soft piles of decaying leaves.*

24

Without the anchor of deep roots, the trees would fall over, but rain forest trees are held up by the supporting buttress roots that grow out from their trunks.

▲ *The buttress roots of giant trees begin about 15 feet (4.5 m) above the ground and extend downward for the same distance.*

▼ *This beautiful green anole is one of about 165 different species of anole lizards that live in the South American rain forest.*

The fight for light

Many rain forest trees produce large seeds, with enough food inside for their saplings to reach three feet (0.9 m) or more. Once this food runs out, a sapling may sit in the shade for years without growing an inch. It must wait until a tall tree dies and falls, opening up space for it to grow into the canopy.

What's for dinner?

Because of the shortage of plant life on the forest floor, many creatures live off what falls down from the canopy and the understory. Beetles, termites, and other insects eat leaf litter and wood. These creatures in turn are eaten by larger insects, spiders, lizards, and mammals.

Ants are the most successful insects of the forest floor. There are many different species, but they all live and work together in communities that are thousands strong.

Leafcutters

Leafcutters are the champion weight lifters of the ant world. Every day, they cut segments from canopy leaves and carry them all the way down to their underground nests. Leafcutter ants can lift leaf segments that are over 50 times their own weight! They do not eat the leaves they collect. Instead, they chew them up and spit them out as mulch. They live on a fungus that grows on the mulch.

Few things can be more awe-inspiring than a column of army ants. Armed with painful stings and powerful jaws, these tiny creatures march across the forest floor, devouring nearly everything in their path. Many forest birds take advantage of the chaos the ants cause, following close behind the columns of ants and picking off the insects they disturb.

FANTASTIC FACTS

● Only five percent of sunlight reaches the forest floor.

● The forest floor is home to centipedes eight inches (20 cm) long.

● A column of army ants can contain over 20 million insects.

Mammals of the forest floor

One of the most common mammals of the forest floor is the agouti. This rabbit-sized rodent has a plentiful supply of brazil nuts all to itself. No other animal can bite through the hard shells of the nuts.

The agouti hides its brazil nuts in underground stores then digs them up when food is scarce. Sometimes it forgets where its secret larder is, and a few of the seeds sprout.

The agouti is the only animal in the rain forest with a strong enough bite to break a brazil nut shell.

Peccaries, small relatives of the farmyard pig, are well suited to life on the forest floor. The animals wander around in large, noisy groups of up to 50, using their long snouts and tusks to dig around in the leaf litter for seeds, fallen fruit, and roots.

At over six feet (1.8 m) long, the tapir is one of the largest creatures in the forest. Its long snout ends in a short trunk. The tapir eats leaves, shoots, and buds. It likes to feed near streams, rivers, and lakes. A good swimmer, the tapir can escape into the water if a predator appears.

The most dangerous animal hunters of the forest floor are jaguars and poisonous snakes. But people hunt here as well, for food and for sport. Native peoples use poison blow darts to shoot down birds and monkeys from the branches.

▲ *Tapirs are shy creatures. They are hunted by jaguars—and people.*

◄ *Poison for the blow darts is taken from the most poisonous animal in the forest, the golden arrow frog.*

29

Life in a tree near you

Next time you pass a tree in your neighborhood, think about the things you have learned in this book. If you look hard enough, you will see that the trees around you are also full of life.

How do the trees in your neighborhood spread their seeds? If they produce fruit, nuts, or acorns, you can be sure that animals spread the seeds. Light, feathery seeds, on the other hand, mean that the wind carries the seeds.

Birds are the creatures that you are most likely to see in your neighborhood trees. Birds hop from branch to branch, searching for fruit, berries, insects, and grubs. They raise their families in trees as well, either in nests, hidden among the leaves, or in hollowed-out holes in the trunk of the tree.

▲ *Like the toucan, the woodpecker makes its nest inside a tree's trunk.*

If you have a garden with a tree in it, why not ask your parents to put up a nesting box? If some birds decide to lay their eggs in it, you will be able to watch the parent birds as they fly back and forth, carrying worms and insects for their growing chicks.

In the fall, you may see squirrels leaping nimbly from branch to branch in search of nuts for the winter storage.

There is plenty of life to see in every tree, all you have to do is look!

◄ *House cats are related to the ocelots and jaguars of the rain forest. They too are predators. They hunt for birds in the trees and mice on the ground.*

31

Words to know

camouflage Colors and patterns that help an animal to blend in with its surroundings.
epiphytes Plants that dangle their roots in the air.
fertilization When the male part of a plant or animal joins the female part.
leaf litter Decaying leaves.
mammals Warm-blooded, hairy animals that raise their young on mother's milk.

nectar Sweet food made by plants to tempt insects.
nutrients Plant food, found in soil and leaf litter.
pollen Yellow powder made by the male part of a flower.
predator An animal that hunts other animals for food.
prehensile tail A tail that can grasp hold of things.
prey An animal that is eaten by another animal.

Index

agouti 6, 28
anole 26
ant 26-27
bromeliad 6, 10, 11
butterfly 6, 18
drip-tip leaves 10
epiphyte 11
food chain 15
frog 7, 8, 10, 16, 23, 24, 29
fruit 12-14

fruit bat 12
harpy eagle 6, 14
hummingbird 14
jaguar 4, 6, 23, 29
katydid 12
liana 20, 21
leaf litter 24
monkey 4, 6, 10, 13, 16, 17, 20
parrot 15
peccary 6, 28

poison 12, 23, 29
seed 12, 26, 28
sloth 6, 7, 8, 9, 14
snake 6, 18, 22, 29
strangler fig 6, 10, 18
tamandua 6, 21
tapir 28, 29
tarantula 24
termite 21, 26
toucan 6, 22